USING
HEARING AIDS

BY HARRIET BRUNDLE

Kidhaven
PUBLISHING

HUMAN BODY HELPERS

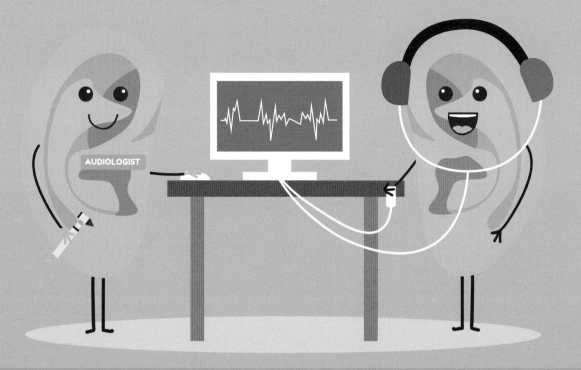

Published in 2019 by
KidHaven Publishing, an Imprint of Greenhaven Publishing, LLC
353 3rd Avenue
Suite 255
New York, NY 10010

Designer: Danielle Rippengill
Editor: Kirsty Holmes

Photo credits: *All images are courtesy of Shutterstock.com, unless
otherwise specified. With thanks to Getty Images, Thinkstock Photo
and iStockphoto. Front Cover & 1 – Pogorelova Olga, Beatriz Gascon
J, NikaMooni, Milan M. Images used on every spread – grmarc, Beatriz
Gascon J, NikaMooni, Pogorelova Olga. 2 – lenoleum. 5 – Neonic Flower,
ann131313. 7 & 8 – lenoleum. 9 – jehsomwang. 10 – ann131313. 11 –
ehsomwang. 14 – EstherQueen999. 15 – lenoleum. 16 – paradesign. 17 &
20 – Iuliia Saenkova. 20 – vladwel. 21 – Elvetica. 22 – What's My Name.*

All facts, statistics, web addresses and URLs in this book were verified
as valid and accurate at time of writing. No responsibility for any
changes to external websites or references can be accepted by either
the author or publisher.

Cataloging-in-Publication Data

Names: Brundle, Harriet.
Title: Using hearing aids / Harriet Brundle.
Description: New York : KidHaven Publishing, 2019. | Series: Human
body helpers | Includes glossary and index.
Identifiers: ISBN 9781534529519 (pbk.) | ISBN 9781534529533 (library
bound) | ISBN 9781534529526 (6 pack) | ISBN 9781534529540
(ebook)
Subjects: LCSH: Hearing aids for children–Juvenile literature. Hearing
impaired children–Juvenile literature.
Classification: LCC RF300.B77 2019 | DDC 617.8′9–dc23

Printed in the United States of America

CPSIA compliance information: Batch #BW19KL: For further information contact Greenhaven
Publishing LLC, New York, New York at 1-844-317-7404.

Please visit our website, www.greenhavenpublishing.com. For a free
color catalog of all our high-quality books, call toll free 1-844-317-7404
or fax 1-844-317-7405.

CONTENTS

Words that look like **this** can be found in the glossary on page 24.

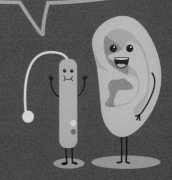

YOUR EARS

EARS ... WE ALL HAVE THEM. BUT WHY DO WE NEED THEM?

We use our ears to hear sounds around us. Our ears send this information to our brains. Our ears are made up of three parts: the outer, middle, and inner ear.

Hi! I'm Eric Ear and I've got the important job of helping you to hear.

We have an ear on each side of our heads. This makes it easier for our brains to know where a sound is coming from. Having two ears also helps us hear sounds on either side of us clearly.

Our ears also help us to keep our **balance**.

WHAT ARE HEARING AIDS?
HEARING AIDS ARE SMALL <u>DEVICES</u> THAT HELP US TO HEAR MORE CLEARLY.

Hi! I'm Harry Hearing Aid and I'm here to help.

Hearing aids fit around or inside our ears and are powered with **<u>batteries</u>**. There are different types of hearing aids.

Behind-the-ear hearing aids have a small plastic device that sits around the top of your ear and behind it.

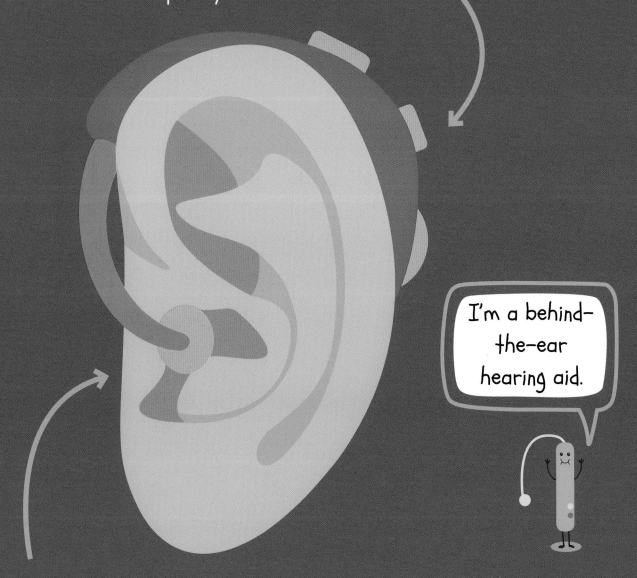

This part is attached to a wire that has a small, plastic piece on the end that fits into your ear.

In-the-ear hearing aids are less **visible** than behind-the-ear hearing aids, because they fit straight into your ear and do not have the extra piece of plastic behind your ear.

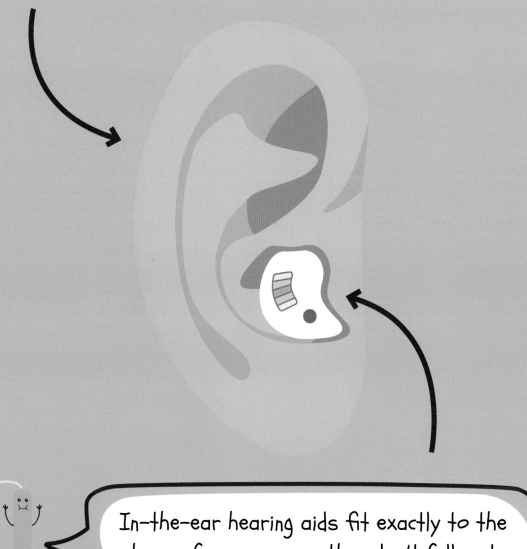

In-the-ear hearing aids fit exactly to the shape of your ear so they don't fall out.

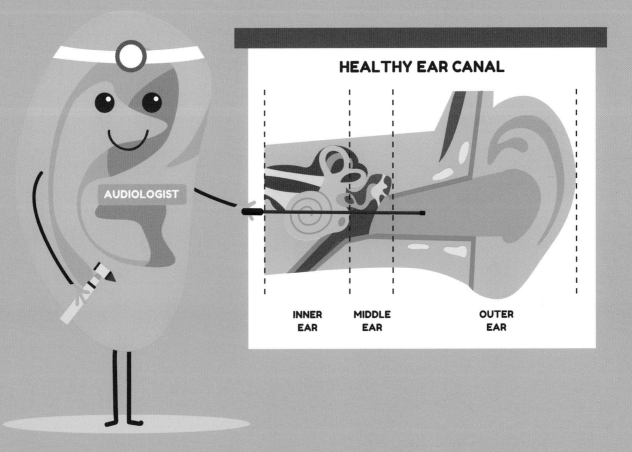

A person who helps with your hearing is called an audiologist (say: aw-dee-ah-lo-gist).

AUDIOLOGIST

HEALTHY EAR CANAL

INNER EAR

MIDDLE EAR

OUTER EAR

Children often start with a behind-the-ear hearing aid. However, each type of hearing aid has different **benefits** and one type might suit your needs better than another.

WHY MIGHT I NEED HEARING AIDS?

YOU MIGHT NOTICE THAT YOU CAN'T HEAR AS CLEARLY AS YOU WOULD LIKE. It might be that you cannot hear when someone is speaking to you or that you struggle to hear when watching the television.

You might notice you can only hear louder sounds.

There are lots of different reasons why you might need extra help to hear. It could be that part of your ear is not working as it should be, or it could be because of an illness.

EXOSTOSES EAR CANAL

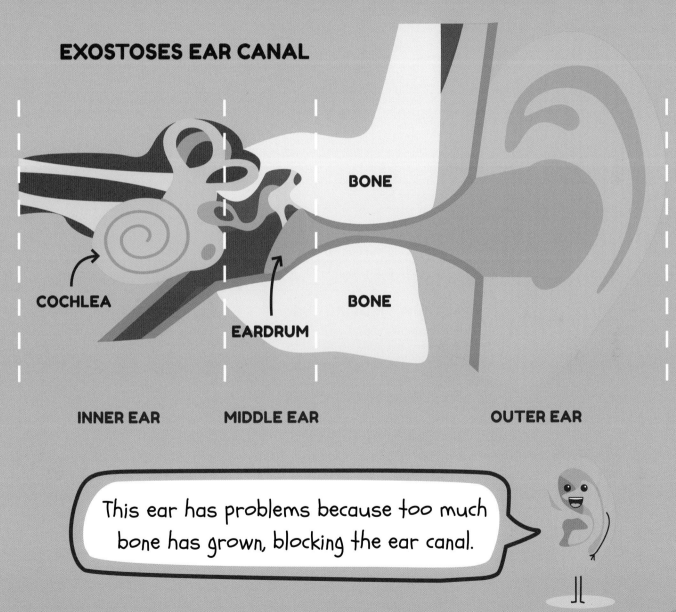

COCHLEA

BONE

EARDRUM

BONE

INNER EAR

MIDDLE EAR

OUTER EAR

This ear has problems because too much bone has grown, blocking the ear canal.

HOW DO HEARING AIDS WORK?

With a behind-the-ear hearing aid, the hearing aid will pick up sounds around you through a small **microphone**. The sounds are then sent through to an **amplifier**.

Hi, I'm Harry and I'm your new hearing aid.

Hi, Harry. I'm Eric. It's great to meet you!

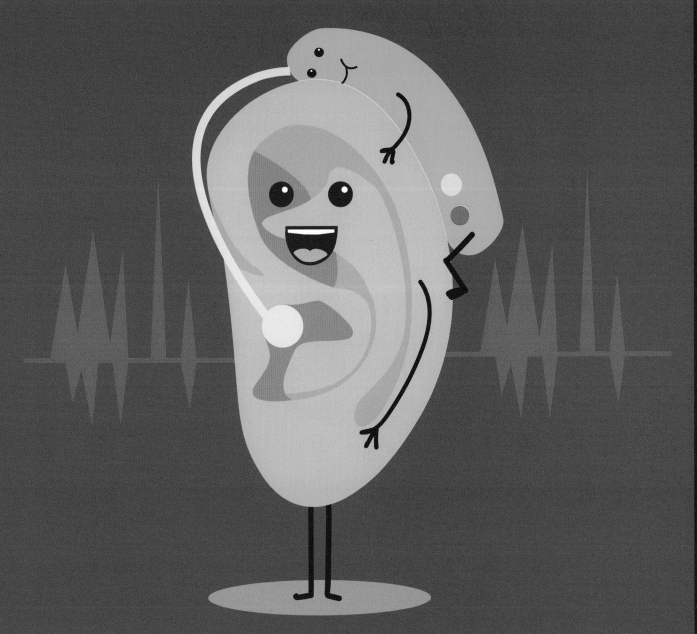

The sounds are sent through to your ear by a small speaker in the opening to your ear. The different parts of the hearing aid work together to make the sound as clear as possible.

WHAT HAPPENS IF I NEED HEARING AIDS?

If you're finding it difficult to hear, the first step is usually to go to see the doctor.

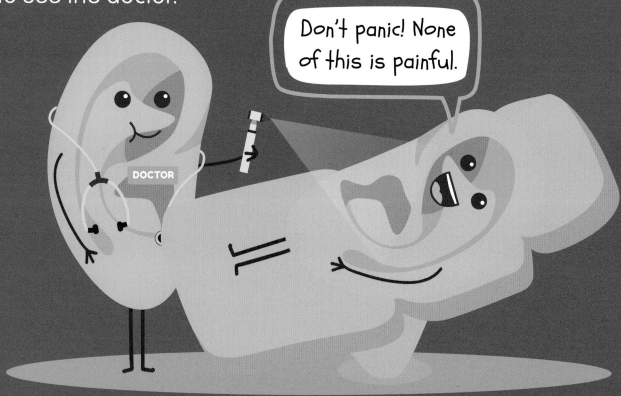

They might have a look in your ears or do other tests to try to find out how well you can hear.

Your doctor might send you to see an audiologist.

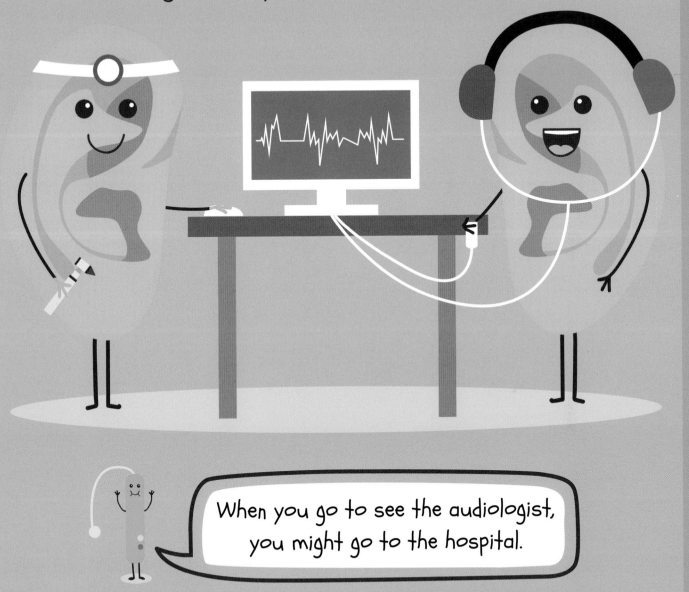

When you go to see the audiologist, you might go to the hospital.

The audiologist may do more tests to check your hearing. You might need a hearing aid for one ear, or both.

If the audiologist thinks that you need hearing aids, they will take **impressions** of your ears. This is so they can make your hearing aids fit your ears perfectly.

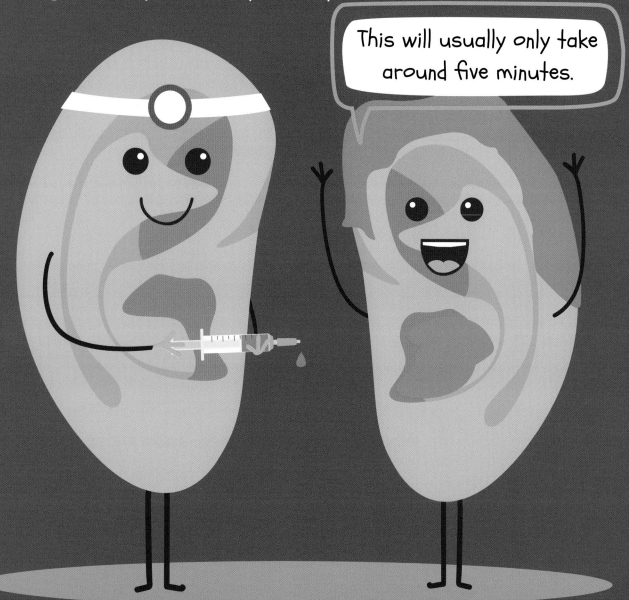

This will usually only take around five minutes.

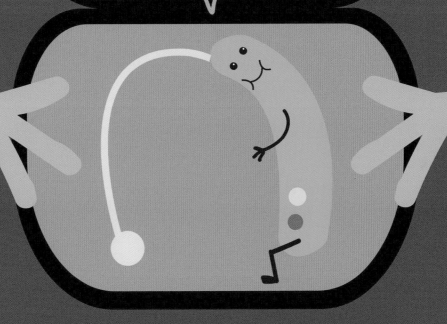

The impressions are sent away and made into hearing aids. Once they're ready, you'll go back to see the audiologist to get your hearing aids.

WHAT TO EXPECT

It might take some time to get used to the difference your hearings aids make.

Try your hearing aids somewhere quiet to start with.

The audiologist might suggest you wear them for a short time to start with, then build up to wearing them for longer each day.

For the first few days after you have had your hearing aid fitted, they might feel strange. Don't worry, after a while you'll become used to the feeling of wearing your hearing aids.

Don't worry, Eric, it won't be long until you're used to me.

DOS AND DON'TS

DO make sure you take good care of your hearing aids. Keep them in a safe case when you're not wearing them so they can't be damaged.

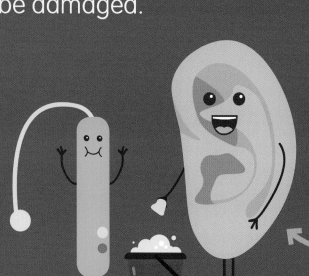

DO make sure you keep your hearing aids clean by cleaning them every day.

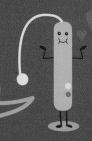

Please look after me!

DON'T let your hearing aids get wet. Remember to take them out before you get in the shower or bath.

DON'T forget to check your hearing aids each day to make sure they are working properly.

LIFE WITH HEARING AIDS

Once you start wearing hearing aids, you might need to take more care when playing sports to make sure they don't come out or get damaged.

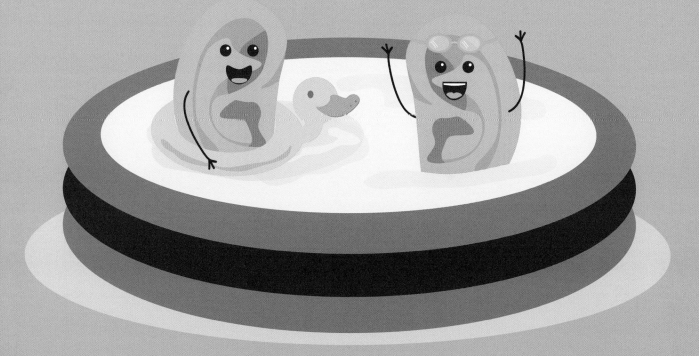

If you go swimming, you'll need to remember to take me out then, too!

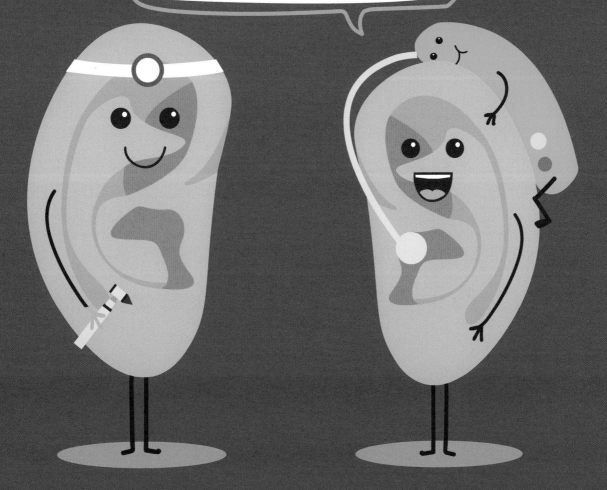

You'll need to make sure you go for all of your hearing aid appointments. The audiologist might make a new impression and will check your ears and your hearing. They will also make sure your hearing aids are working as they should be.

GLOSSARY

AMPLIFIER   an electronic device that increases the power of a signal

BALANCE   being in a steady position so you do not fall

BATTERIES   devices that are a source of power

BENEFITS   to gain from something

DEVICES   a piece of equipment

IMPRESSIONS   a mold of the shape of something

MICROPHONE   used to record or send out sounds

VISIBLE   able to be seen

INDEX